TERENCE CONRAN

ESSENTIAL COLOUR

THE BACK TO BASICS GUIDE TO HOME DESIGN, DECORATION & FURNISHING

conran
OCTOPUS

Contents

14

Understanding Colour

Colour Schemes

Practical Colour

INTRODUCTION

UNDERSTANDING COLOUR

COLOUR

COLOUR SCHEMES

PRACTICAL COLOUR

Introduction

In the modern world, we take colour for granted. It is everywhere: in newspapers and magazines, on packaging, on our computer screens; you can buy coloured fridges, cars, toothbrushes and crockery; you can print out your own colour photos using coloured inks.

When you walk into a clothes shop and see stacks of identical T-shirts, you do not expect the coloured ones to cost more than the white ones, or the green ones to be more expensive than the blue. This was not always the case. Despite the riot of colour in the natural world, our ability to reproduce what we saw around us in dyes and pigments was strictly limited for a very long time. For centuries, the colours in everyday use came chiefly from plants and earth, which resulted in a soft, muted palette. Brighter, stronger colours, such as cochineal, the red dye made from beetles, or pure blue, derived from the rare and costly mineral lapis lazuli, were harder to come by and often very expensive. Even a reliable black was hard to achieve.

Technical advances in the nineteenth century, along with the widening of trade routes, began to increase the range of possibilities for using colour. In the mid-nineteenth century, chemists developed the first synthetic dyes; a few decades later the development of lithography brought the first colour reproductions within the reach of the ordinary household.

It was only in the second half of the twentieth century, however, that colour really exploded into everyday life. Today's world of cheap and cheerful colour comes from the growth of the synthetics industry in the post-war period, which ensured that colour would never be available only to the

ABOVE: COLOURED LIGHT IS VERY ATMOSPHERIC. THIS BACKLIT GLASS SHELF EMITS A SOFT BLUE GLOW.

LEFT: BRIGHT LACQUERED KITCHEN CABINETS ECHO THE COLOUR OF THE OUTDOOR SEATING. STRONG COLOUR NEEDS PLENTY OF BREATHING SPACE.

continued

Introduction

wealthy again. Ever since the arrival of the first newspaper colour supplement and the first colour TVs, colour has been firmly embedded in mass consumer culture.

Despite this colour saturation – or perhaps because of it – the pigment manufactured in the largest quantities today remains white. Many people display a certain hesitancy when it comes to using colour in their homes, with neutral schemes – safe natural tones, whites and off-whites – all too often the norm. It would seem that rather than being spoiled for choice, when it comes to being imaginative with colour, we are often daunted by it.

There is nothing wrong with neutral or natural schemes, and a predominance of white as a background in many of today's interiors reflects an understandable desire to enhance space and light, two of the elements we prize most in contemporary décor. At the same time, there is a misconception that colourful surroundings are tiring to live in, which ignores the fact that the typical office environment, with its off-white walls and sea of grey carpeting, is a drain on the spirits and something most of us would rather escape from.

Fear of 'getting it wrong' is what makes many people stick to the safe and expected when they are choosing how to decorate their homes. It is true that working with colour takes a degree of skill, and that trial and error may come into it. Even for the most hesitant, though, there are ways of introducing colour to the home that can help to build up confidence and expertise in colour handling without running the risk of making an expensive mistake.

We are lucky to be living at a time when colours of every description are available in paint, fabric, wallpaper, flooring, and almost every other decorative element. To turn your back on colour altogether is to miss the opportunity to explore its unique ability to evoke atmosphere and feeling, to lift our spirits and express *joie de vivre*. Colour is literally the spice of life.

ABOVE: SOFT FURNISHINGS PROVIDE THE OPPORTUNITY TO INTRODUCE COLOUR TO THE INTERIOR IN UNDERSTATED WAYS.

RIGHT: HIDDEN COLOUR: DRAWERS PAINTED MARINE BLUE CONCEALED BEHIND WHITE FLUSH PANELS.

INTRODUCTION

UNDERSTANDING COLOUR

COLOUR

SCHEMES

PRACTICAL

COLOUR

How colour works

Colour is a function of how our eyes perceive light. Radiated by the sun, light travels to us on different wavelengths, each corresponding to a colour in the spectrum. Grass looks green because it has absorbed all the wavelengths except the green, which is reflected back to our eyes. Although we are capable of making subtle distinctions between millions of different colours and tones, we are only able to see a portion of the spectrum; the extremes – ultraviolet and infrared – are invisible to us.

There are many ways of depicting colour relationships, but the most familiar and perhaps the most useful in decoration, is the artist's colour wheel. In this working model, the three primary colours are red, yellow and blue, which cannot be reproduced by mixing any other colours. Secondary colours, made by mixing two adjacent primaries are orange (red and yellow), green (yellow and blue) and purple (blue and red). When these colours are arranged in a circle, those that sit opposite one another – red and green, blue and orange, and yellow and violet – are said to be 'complementary'. Pairings of complementary colours in different tones form the basis of many decorative schemes.

ABOVE: BLUE AND GREEN ARE OFTEN FOUND IN COMBINATION WITH EACH OTHER IN THE NATURAL WORLD.

RIGHT: EACH COLOUR IN THE SPECTRUM CORRESPONDS TO A DIFFERENT WAVELENGTH OF LIGHT.

Colour language

Every colour brings with it a raft of associations, some historical, some cultural, and others much more personal and subjective. What colours mean and what language they speak has a great deal to do with this wider picture. Historically, red was thought to be an appropriate colour for walls in rooms where pictures were displayed. Blue was believed to repel flies and was often found in dairies and kitchens. Around the world there are some surprising differences of interpretation: in the West, for example, brides have traditionally worn white since Queen Victoria set the trend in the nineteenth century, while in Asia white is the colour of mourning.

These associations become more subtle when colours are used together. A particular palette or combination of shades may summon up the specific period in decoration when it was widely used, which can be an instant way of giving a retro scheme authenticity; or it may evoke a culture or location where such colours are prevalent. In this context, a palette of bleached blues and greys might suggest airy Scandinavian style décor, while a hot spicy combination of orange, pink, red and brown has more of a Mexican flavour. Added to the mix are our own very personal preferences, which may date back to childhood memories.

ABOVE: PINKS, PURPLES AND REDS, USED IN COMBINATION, SUGGEST A MORE EASTERN STYLE OF DECORATION.

LEFT: A COOL NATURAL PALETTE EVOKES A MID-CENTURY MODERN AESTHETIC, TYPICAL OF CONTEMPORARY SCANDINAVIAN DESIGN.

Getting inspired

Getting inspired by colour means rediscovering a sense of wonder in a world that is increasingly saturated with colour in all possible tones and shades. Children are naturally attracted to bright colourful things and some people retain a delight in colour for its own sake all their lives. Others have to work a little harder to re-acquaint themselves with the pleasure colour can bring.

Most of us are drawn to certain families of colours more than others, a preference that is often displayed in our wardrobes. Other sources of inspiration can come from the types of places we like to go on holiday, or the combinations that are depicted in the art of superb colourists such as Vincent van Gogh, Henri Matisse, Patrick Heron and Howard Hodgkin.

Yet you do not have to go very far or spend hours of research to come up with colour ideas. Instead, it is all about learning to look. A walk in the park on a spring morning, a trip to a local market heaped with fresh produce, or a day at the beach can help you to see the world afresh. When you really start to take notice you will find inspiration in a host of places: movie stills, book jackets, product packaging, painted shopfronts – whatever catches your eye and gives you a thrill.

ABOVE: INSPIRATION IS EVERYWHERE. THESE BOBBINS OF BRIGHTLY COLOURED SILK THREAD ARE A FEAST FOR THE EYES.

RIGHT: NATURE IS AN UNBEATABLE SOURCE OF COLOUR IDEAS, AS SHOWN BY THIS VIBRANT PAIRING OF ORANGE POPPIES AND BLUE CORNFLOWERS.

Warm colours

Red, orange and yellow, the warm colours of the spectrum, are said to be 'advancing', which means that they attract attention and jump out at you. This is because warm colours correspond to the longer wavelengths of light and demand more adjustment from our eyes, a physical stimulus we interpret as excitement, alarm or arousal. In decorative terms, these colours make great accents, while as background shades they are cosy and intimate, making the walls of a room appear to draw in.

Red

The colour of strong feeling – love, anger and celebration – red also signifies a high degree of danger and alert – the poisonous berry, the stop sign, the splash of blood. Red speeds things up; in the wrong circumstances it can also over-stimulate. Traditionally, red – specifically in the form of fabric hangings – was often chosen as the backdrop for picture rooms and galleries in grand houses. Red adds welcome warmth to a decorative scheme, particularly if the quality of natural light is chilly or poor.

Pink

A lighter variant of red, pink has a strong association with femininity. Delicate, flattering and luxurious in the right context, it can also appear insipid or cloying if not carefully used. An earthy pink, the colour of unfinished plaster, makes a relaxing and comfortable background colour without specific feminine overtones.

ABOVE: AGAINST A SOOTHING GREY BACKGROUND, THE ORANGE-RED LAMPSHADE STRIKES A STRONG COLOUR ACCENT, ECHOED BY THE FLATWEAVE RUG.

LEFT: RED IS AN ADVANCING COLOUR, WHICH MAKES IT WARM AND INTIMATE IN LARGE DOSES.

Continued

Warm colours

Orange

From gentle tones of pale apricot and peach to strong, clear shades bursting with the warmth of the sun, orange fosters a sense of well-being and happiness. It is also associated with modernity. Rarely found in historic interiors, orange first became popular in the decorative schemes of Art Nouveau in the late 1800s, and Art Deco in the 1920s and 1930s. It saw a more recent revival in the pop-inspired fashions and designs of the 1960s and 1970s.

Like red, in its purest and most intense form, orange is an energizing, eye-catching shade, said to be the first colour that babies can recognize. More muted, earthier tones of burnt orange or brick red make hospitable, soothing backdrops redolent of warmer climates.

Yellow

Inherently optimistic, uplifting and cheerful, yellow strikes a positive note without being overly demanding. In decoration, bright pure yellow was unknown before the invention of chrome yellow at the beginning of the nineteenth century; previously yellow had been produced using the earth pigment ochre.

From pale buttermilk, through sharp citrus to rich, warm golden shades, yellow naturally lightens and brightens any room. In a kitchen, it can promote a feeling of hospitality, but it can also create a more stately and classical mood as a background for living areas. Yellow, though, can be notoriously difficult to get right. You may need to experiment to find the right shade, which will depend on existing conditions of natural light.

ABOVE: YELLOW IS A VERY CHEERFUL COLOUR AND LOOKS BEST WHERE THE QUALITY OF NATURAL LIGHT IS GOOD, AS IT IS IN THIS TOP LIT LIVING/DINING AREA.

RIGHT: WARM AND HOSPITABLE, ORANGE IS A PUNCHY COLOUR WITH A MODERN EDGE. THE COPPER LAMPSHADES AND TANGERINE SPLASHBACK WORK WELL TOGETHER.

Green

If red speeds things up, its complementary colour green slows things down. Neither a warm colour nor a cool one, it occupies the middle of the spectrum and is the most restful colour of all because our eyes have to make the least adjustment to see it. This may well be the reason why green has long been considered beneficial for the eyesight – blinds made of green fabric, green eyeshades and green lampshades were all traditional means of screening strong light.

Healing, soothing and refreshing, green is naturally associated with fertility and growth. The association with nature and the landscape is underscored by the many common names we have for different shades: everything from lime and mint to forest, olive and leaf. But green has its negative associations, too – with illness, jealousy and betrayal, and the greenish cast of fluorescent light is very unflattering.

While green is unlikely to make your pulse race, it is indispensable in decorative schemes simply because it works well with so many other colours. Mixed with blues, it forms the basis of many marine or seashore palettes; combined with reds it can have a vibrant folk-art quality or a pretty countrified look straight out of a cottage garden. Lime green is edgier and more modern; jade and celadon are elegant and sophisticated with oriental overtones. As a background, calm and sombre deep green has traditionally been the colour for a library or study.

ABOVE: SHUTTERS AND WOODWORK PAINTED LEAF GREEN HAVE A FRESH COUNTIFIED LOOK IN A SIMPLE RUSTIC INTERIOR.

LEFT: GREEN, WHICH OCCUPIES THE MIDDLE OF THE VISIBLE SPECTRUM, IS INHERENTLY RESTFUL AND MAKES A GOOD BACKGROUND IN A ROOM DEDICATED TO RELAXATION.

Cool colours

The short wavelengths of light correspond to blues and violets, colours that are inherently soothing and distancing – think of the blue of the horizon, or distant hills. Cool colours are naturally space-enhancing, airy and expansive. However, where light conditions are poor, or in north-facing locations, they can be inhospitable and chilly, even gloomy.

Blue

There is an incredible variety of blues, from pale powder blue to deep intense indigo, from edgy lavender and blue-grey to turquoise and blue-green. Depending on the particular shade, it can be elegant and fresh, or cheery and domestic. An essentially restful and contemplative colour, blue can be used in large doses without appearing too dominant. Its association with water makes it a popular choice for bathrooms.

Blue works well with many other colours but an especially evocative pairing is blue and white. This combination became popular in the seventeenth century when blue and white Chinese porcelain first began to arrive in the West. Nowadays blue and white has a more homely quality, suggestive of everyday household furnishings such as striped tea towels and mattress ticking.

Violet

At the extreme end of the spectrum, blue bleeds into violet. Pale shades of violet can be very sophisticated and refined. Harder to handle, is purple, with its strong overtones of secular and religious power and authority.

ABOVE: BLUE IS A POPULAR CHOICE FOR BATHROOM DÉCOR. THESE SOFT SEA BLUE-GREEN WALLS ARE AIRY AND RESTFUL.

RIGHT: THE MOODIEST AND MOST DRAMATIC OF ALL BLUES IS INDIGO, WITH ITS RICH AND SOULFUL QUALITY.

Neutrals

The neutral shades of white, grey and black – what one might call non-colours – are crucial in decorative schemes, supplying not only essential breathing space but also tonality and definition. While there are exceptions, all-neutral schemes run the risk of being dull and uninspiring. Instead, they are often more effective when they serve as a foil for stronger colours.

White

For many centuries white was strictly a utility colour – lime-based distemper was typically the no-nonsense backdrop of service areas. All that changed with the arrival of electricity and, in the 1930s, all-white schemes, featuring the new brilliant titanium white, became the height of fashion in the hands of society decorators. Nowadays, white is much associated with Modernism and minimal styles of décor, as well as being a popular fail-safe choice for those who are uncertain about colour. Magnolia, a warmish off-white, has been a best-selling paint colour for many years.

White is a family of shades, ranging from ivory, pearl and cream to chalk, linen and biscuit. Choosing the right white means thinking about the quality of natural light: sunny rooms can take the cooler whites, whereas warmer or creamier whites work better in areas where natural light is poor. Many paint manufacturers add a touch of blue to their standard white paints to give added 'brilliance', but the result can be a little glaring.

ABOVE: IN THE CONTEMPORARY INTERIOR, WHITE IS ONE OF THE MOST POPULAR CHOICES FOR BACKGROUNDS, MAKING THE MOST OF LIGHT AND SPACE.

LEFT: WHITES VARY IN TONE AND GREAT CARE HAS BEEN TAKEN IN THIS KITCHEN TO MATCH TILES AND PAINTWORK WITH CABINETS AND THE STOVE.

Continued

Neutrals

Grey

Although grey sounds dreary and lacklustre, the epitome of a rainy day, it actually forms a very useful family of shades. Grey can be both a great mediator and a subtle and refined background in its own right.

Grey ranges from the palest whisper of smoke and gentle dove grey to a deep battleship shade that packs graphic punch. Silvery blue-greys are cool and refined, while warmer mushroom tones have great compatibility with earthy colour schemes. In many interiors, grey is evident in the choice of materials – the dull lustre of brushed stainless steel, for example, or the classic pale colour of natural stone.

Black

The absence of colour or light, black can be used as a dramatic element in decoration. With the exception of bathrooms tiled in black slate or ceramic tiles, the use of black as a background colour is understandably rare. More often, black is used as a defining accent or graphic contrast that underscores architectural and decorative detail – the black marble worktop in a neutral kitchen, for example, or the black-stained beams criss-crossing the ceilings of a country cottage. In combination with white, black has a crisp, formal quality. Black and white chequered flooring is a time-honoured classic.

ABOVE: IN THE RIGHT SETTING, GREY MAKES A SUBTLE AND SOPHISTICATED BACKGROUND, HERE COMPLEMENTING THE STONE FIREPLACE AND WOODEN FLOOR.

RIGHT: BLACK AND WHITE MAKE A GRAPHIC AND DYNAMIC COMBINATION. GREY WALLS MEDIATE BETWEEN THE TWO AND AVOID ANY RISK OF STARKNESS.

Naturals

Before industrialisation, pigments and dyes were derived exclusively from animal, vegetable or mineral sources. Since the ingredients that produced the strongest, most vibrant colours tended to be the rarest and most expensive, the ordinary or everyday palette was somewhat soft and muted. Today, we use the term 'natural' to describe a range of earthy shades, from light biscuit tones to dark chocolate brown.

In many interiors, the natural palette is more evident in the choice of materials than in applied decoration such as paintwork or soft furnishings. The subtle colours of wood, stone and earth convey a quiet sense of integrity and longevity. These natural materials also age sympathetically, which adds a certain mellowness and depth of character to a scheme.

Using a natural palette effortlessly conveys a country mood, serving as a connection between an interior and the surrounding landscape, but it can also be the basis for a more sophisticated and sleek urban look. The main risk of using neutrals is creating a bland overall effect. Sharpened with black, freshened with white or offset with vivid accents of strong colour, a natural palette comes to life. Unrelieved by such contrasts, it can be downright uninspiring and monotonous – a sea of beige.

ABOVE: AN EXPOSED BRICK WALL AND STRIPPED FLOORBOARDS ADD A DEPTH OF CHARACTER TO A CONVERTED LOFT.

LEFT: WHILE A NATURAL PALETTE IS OFTEN ASSOCIATED WITH COUNTRY DÉCOR, IT WORKS WELL IN MODERN INTERIORS, TOO, WHERE THE EMPHASIS IS ON MATERIAL CHARACTER.

Continued

Naturals

Brown

One shade you will not find on a colour wheel is brown, but there is plenty of it in nature, from the bark of trees and outcrops of stone to the soil itself. As anyone who has ever played about with a paint box will appreciate, brown is what results when you mix more than two colours together. The precise shade will depend on the colours that have gone into the mix, with tawny or reddish browns, for example, containing a greater proportion of warm colours. Enclosing without being overly insistent, and sombre without being depressing, shades of brown are reassuring and incredibly versatile.

We can tolerate quite large doses of brown in the interior partly because earth pigments are so universal and timeless and partly because materials such as timber, stone, brick and clay are so familiar in the construction of buildings. A converted city loft might feature exposed brick walls and wooden floorboards; an old country house may have interiors panelled in oak darkened by time – what both have in common is a dominant use of brown. Where brown is delivered through the use of materials, it will be inherently lively. Unlike flat colour, the grain of wood, tonal variations of natural stone and the mottled appearance of brick display great depth.

ABOVE: THE EARTHY COLOURS OF STONE, WOOD AND TERRACOTTA ARE NATURALLY ENLIVENED BY THE VARIATIONS IN GRAINING AND SURFACE PATTERN.

RIGHT: PLENTY OF WHITE KEEPS A NATURAL SCHEME FRESH, LIGHT AND BREEZY, IN KEEPING WITH ITS COUNTRY SETTING.

INTRODUCTION
UNDERSTANDING COLOUR
COLOUR SCHEMES
PRACTICAL COLOUR

Basic considerations

Colour is more affordable and available than ever before. Today, we are literally spoiled for choice, which can be a daunting prospect when you are trying to devise a decorative scheme. Personal taste naturally comes into it, but other issues have a role to play.

- The 'aspect' of a particular room, that is, the direction in which it faces, has a great impact on the quality of natural light. This is a key consideration when choosing colours for an interior. Use warm colours for dull or chilly rooms that face north or east, and cool colours for bright rooms that face south or west.
- When planning a colour scheme, it is important to think about the function and ambience of a room, or what the room is used for and whether you want to create a relaxing mood or an energizing one. Hard-working areas such as kitchens, for example, may require more subtle or neutral colour schemes to aid concentration.
- Think about introducing vibrant splashes of colour to halls, stairs and entrances, as well as to small, self-contained rooms such as cloakrooms. Because these are areas where we do not linger for long, there is less risk of growing tired of a strong colour or of being overwhelmed by it.
- If at all possible, try to plan a colour scheme for your home as a whole. You do not have to repeat the same colours everywhere, but it is a good idea if there is a degree of unity – the same colour flooring, for example.

LEFT: A BACKLIT BLUE PANEL ON THE SIDE OF A BATHTUB AND MARINE BLUE MOSAIC WALLS EVOKE A SUITABLY WATERY ATMOSPHERE IN A BATHROOM.

FAR LEFT: A GRAPHIC DISPLAY OF FRAMED BLACK AND WHITE PHOTOGRAPHS AND PRINTS PACKS EXTRA PUNCH ARRANGED ON AN ACID YELLOW WALL.

Mood boards

Professional designers and decorators often assemble mood or sample boards as a preliminary way of focusing their ideas or exploring different directions. The same approach can be usefully adopted by anyone planning a decorative scheme. Creating a mood board allows you to experiment, so you are less likely to be unhappy with the final result.

The first step is to build up a visual library to serve as a source of colour ideas. Keep a scrapbook or desktop file of images that appeal to you – these may include cuttings from magazines, postcards of paintings, packaging, whatever catches your eye. Most mobile phones include fairly sophisticated cameras these days, so it has never been easier to capture a fleeting moment of inspiration when you are out and about – a shop window display, for example, or a garden in full bloom.

The next step is to ground your ideas in reality. Assemble scraps of fabric, paint swatches and other samples to gauge how colours work together. It is best if you can give a rough indication of proportion. If you are planning to accent a pale background colour with a vivid trim, the background colour should occupy more space on the board than the accent. Make sure that you view the sample board under different light conditions, both natural and artificial.

ABOVE: BEFORE YOU MAKE A FINAL SELECTION, GATHER TOGETHER A COLLECTION OF SAMPLES AND SWATCHES TO ASSESS COLOURS IN SITU.

RIGHT: TRY OUT YOUR COLOUR IDEAS ON PAPER FIRST, PARTNERING BACKGROUND SHADES TOGETHER WITH BRIGHTER ACCENT COLOURS.

Ready-made palettes

Using colour successfully takes confidence and a degree of practice. If you are unsure about your colour handling skills, or nervous about using colour altogether, ready-made palettes are the simplest solution.

- Paint manufacturers know that choosing colours can be daunting and many produce brochures that feature palettes that are loosely themed in various ways. Specialist or heritage paint suppliers are a good bet if you are looking for colour combinations that evoke period or retro style décor.
- Interiors features in magazines and newspapers can be an excellent source of ideas. In some cases, the colours in a particular scheme will have been identified and matched with existing products, so the research will have been done for you.
- Most fashion designers have a keen eye for colour and there is no reason why a palette displayed in a season's collection would not work in the home, too.
- Inspiration can come from something you already own or are planning to buy, such as a favourite painting, a rug, or a patterned fabric. You can base a scheme around a number of the colours in the item, choosing a light or neutral colour for backgrounds and more vivid, intense shades as focal points and accents.

ABOVE: BLUE-GREEN BATH LINEN AND SOFT FURNISHINGS COORDINATE WITH ONE OF THE COLOURS DISPLAYED BY THE FLAT-WEAVE RUG.

LEFT: THE PRINT OVER THE FIREPLACE AND THE STRIPY RUG DISPLAY A SIMILAR FAMILY OF COLOURS. THE FAWN BACKGROUND TIES IT ALL NICELY TOGETHER.

Accent

You can learn a great deal about colour without committing yourself to vast effort or expense by playing around with accents. Accents are like fashion accessories, they sharpen or update a look and are easy and affordable to change. If you favour a simple or understated style of décor, either in a particular area or throughout your home, vivid splashes of colour here and there can prevent the overall effect from being too bland or insipid.

Where backgrounds are neutral or natural, almost any strong colour counts as an accent against the blank canvas. Primary colours, of course, are striking, but also secondary and tertiary shades such as orange, turquoise, lavender and lime green. Otherwise, you can exploit the inherent vibrancy of complementary pairs. In a room where the walls are decorated pale yellow, for example, anything bright blue – a vase, a cushion or a framed poster – will sing out with added intensity.

Types of accent

- Smaller-scale soft furnishings, such as cushion covers and throws.
- Pictures, particularly where one colour is most dominant.
- Decorative objects, such as vases and glassware.
- Panels of coloured glass inset into transoms, windows or door frames.
- Cut flowers and indoor plants.
- Everyday kitchen displays, including fresh fruit and vegetables, colourful packaging, coloured crockery, vases, books and basic equipment.

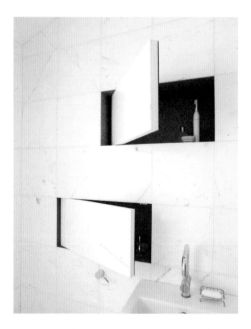

RIGHT: RECESSED STORAGE NICHES PAINTED IN STRONG COLOURS PROVIDE AN ELEMENT OF SURPRISE IN AN OTHERWISE ALL-WHITE SCHEME.

FAR RIGHT: A VIVID GREEN SPLASHBACK AND AN ORANGE LAMPSHADE MAKE CHEERFUL ACCENTS IN A KITCHEN.

Focal point

Using colour as a focal point differs from accent colour chiefly in terms of scale and proportion. Where accent colour can be scattered about, delighting the eye but not dominating the whole picture, treating colour as a focal point inevitably means that you are making more of a statement and bringing colour closer to the foreground.

Types of focal point

- Painting an entire wall in a single colour to create a feature wall is a great way of introducing a sense of vitality into a decorative scheme. It can also help to signal changes of use within an open-plan space, distinguishing an eating area, for example, from an area where food is prepared.
- Choosing a dominant item of furniture or equipment in a strong colour is another way of creating a focal point. A sofa upholstered in a vivid shade or an over-scaled upholstered bedhead can effectively introduce a block of solid colour. Appliances also come in range of colours these days, but bear in mind that you might have tired of the shade in question before your refrigerator or cooker has come to the end of its working life.
- Colour on the floor has great impact and is generally less overwhelming than schemes where the walls are decorated in the same strong shade. Rugs are the easiest way of adding colour at floor level, but many flooring materials, such as vinyl, linoleum and cork, come in a range of shades. For the widest possible choice, think about rubber flooring, which comes in every colour imaginable.

ABOVE: AN ORANGE FEATURE WALL DRAWS THE EYE INTO A SHOWER ENCLOSURE THAT HAS BEEN MINIMALLY SCREENED BY GLAZED PANELS.

LEFT: AN ISLAND UNIT WITH A GREEN FINISH SERVES AS A FOCAL POINT IN A DOUBLE-HEIGHT OPEN-PLAN KITCHEN/LIVING AREA.

Background

One of the legacies of Modernism has been the dominance of the plain white background in interior decoration. This still remains the default option for many people, which is unsurprising. White is a useful way of enhancing space and maximizing natural light, two of the qualities we value most in our homes.

While there is nothing wrong with white or off-white backgrounds, it is a mistake to assume that there is no effort involved in selection. Neutrals can often be amongst the hardest colours to get right. Differences between shades may be subtle, but they still have an impact – a white that might be fresh and invigorating in one setting may look dingy in another.

Rather than choosing a pale shade as a safe option, it is more adventurous and expressive to use background colour in a proactive way as a means of generating mood and atmosphere. Forget pastels, which betray a hesitant toe-in-the-water approach, and go for more positive shades that are full of vitality. Many of the colours that hover on the cusp of one colour and the next, such as blue-green, reddish-orange and lavender have an edgy, luminous quality that can be very appealing.

It is important to be aware that some colours look more intense and saturated when they are covering an entire wall than they do on a chart, so you should always paint a test patch first, preferably on different walls of the room.

ABOVE: NEUTRAL SHADES, SUCH AS THIS PALE GREY, MAKE GOOD BACKGROUNDS, BUT YOU HAVE TO ENSURE THE PRECISE TONE IS RIGHT FOR THE LIGHT CONDITIONS.

RIGHT: BLUE-GREY HAS MORE DEPTH OF CHARACTER AND INHERENT VITALITY THAN A PASTEL BLUE.

Coordination

Basing a decorative scheme on the repetition of a single colour can be very dramatic and powerful. An all-white décor, for example, is theatrical and ethereal, almost other-worldly. At the same time, a little coordination can go a long way – a bathroom where the towels, bathmat, walls and fittings are all in the same colour can look prissy and fussy. Relentless matching can have the odd effect of deadening or neutralizing a colour's impact because the eye sees the same thing wherever it looks. When it is insensitively overdone, coordination falls as flat as the punch-line of a joke that has been repeated too often.

One of the difficulties with colour coordination is that it can be hard to match shades exactly when you are working with different materials. The same red, for example, will look different in a matt carpet weave than it will in a velvety pile because of the textural variation, just as gloss paint differs from emulsion. One way around this problem is to include plenty of plain or neutral surfaces between the coordinated elements to serve as breathing spaces and to make any slight differences of tone less noticeable. This is also a good way of avoiding the risk of claustrophobia, which can occur where foreground and background blur into each other.

LEFT: PAINTING THE CHIMNEYPIECE, PANELLING, WOODWORK AND CHAIR THE SAME SHADE OF WHITE IS AN EFFORTLESS WAY OF ACHIEVING COORDINATION.

FAR LEFT: THE EARTHY COLOUR OF THE WOODEN STOOLS AND FLOORBOARDS HELPS TO GROUND AN ALL-WHITE DÉCOR.

Tones & shades

Rather than strive for precise coordination, a subtler and inherently less risky way of basing a decorative scheme around a single colour is to use different tones and shades of it.

Put simply, the tone of a colour is how light or dark it is, while different shades of the same colour depend on which other colours are in the mix. A 'blue' palette devised according to this approach might include very pale tones contrasted with darker, more graphic ones, along with several shades of blue that have warmer or cooler elements, such as blue-green or grey-blue. A 'pink' palette might range from the palest blush tone to vibrant fuchsia, mediated with an earthier plaster colour.

It is important to mix both tones and shades when thinking of a colour scheme. A palette that merely shows tonal variation will be about as exciting as a paint manufacturer's colour chart, while if you mix too many shades together at once, it can be visually indigestible.

Using tones and shades is a great way of indulging yourself in your favourite colour. It is easier on the eye than coordination, too. As with coordinated schemes, however, plenty of breathing space is essential to avoid an effect that is too stifling or lifeless.

ABOVE: MID-BLUE WALLS ARE SET OFF BY A DEEP BLUE PAINTING IN A SCHEME BASED ON TONES AND SHADES.

RIGHT: A SUBTLE TONAL SCHEME FEATURES A RANGE OF GREYS, FROM THE GALVANIZED POT AND CHROME FITTINGS TO THE SLATE SURROUND AND BROWNISH-GREY WOODWORK.

Harmonious schemes

A step further than combining tones and shades of the same colour is to combine colours that lie close to each other on the colour wheel. These near-neighbours are naturally harmonious, which means that you can achieve a successful result very simply and one that instantly conveys a distinctive mood. A combination of cool colours, such as blues, blue-greens and greys, will be restful and space-enhancing, while a warm palette, based on pinks and reds, or reds and oranges, will be more energetic and enclosing.

It is not all plain sailing, however. As with any colour scheme, you need to play around with tones to get the balance right. A tried and tested strategy is to use light or pale shades on the walls, restrict dark, intense or rich colours to accents and make use of mid-tones elsewhere, as soft furnishings, perhaps. An alternate route is to combine colours that are tonally very similar. In practice this tends to work best when all the colours are very light in tone – blocks of bright solid colour need much more careful handling. Pale blue, pale lavender, light grey and light grey-green conjure up a summery seascape mood, while a palette of buff, cream, pale terracotta and plaster pink has an earthier feel.

LEFT: COOL BLUE AND VIOLET CREATE AN AIRY AND EXPANSIVE EFFECT IN A BEDROOM, COMPLEMENTED BY THE STAINLESS STEEL LAMP AND BEDSIDE TABLE LEGS.

FAR LEFT: WARM, EARTHY COLOURS, RANGING FROM CREAM AND TAN THROUGH ORANGE, OCHRE AND BROWN ARE THE BASIS FOR THIS HARMONIOUS SCHEME.

Complementary schemes

Complementary colours are those that sit opposite each other on the colour wheel – red and green, blue and orange, yellow and violet – and they form the basis of many decorative schemes. In their pure forms, complementary colours create electric combinations where each shade appears to vibrate against the other, vying for attention. A great way of exploiting this characteristic is to use a small amount of one colour to accent the other in the form of a trim or detail. Tonal shades of the same colours are less stimulating, but equally compatible.

Colour mixing can help you appreciate how these partnerships work. Take the example of red and green, a combination that has a long history of use in decoration, such as the pinks and soft greens so typical of chintz. Mixing a little of the red into the green and a little of the green into the red automatically produces a pair of complex, subtle shades that are inherently linked to one another, even if the colours you started with were not perfectly matched in tone or intensity. To build up a family of related colours, add white to create light tones, or more of the complementary to create dark tones.

ABOVE: BLUE AND ORANGE, LIKE ALL COMPLEMENTARY PAIRS, HAVE A NATURAL VIBRANCY. HERE THEY ARE MEDIATED BY PLENTY OF WHITE.

RIGHT: THE TRANSPARENCY OF GLASS GIVES ADDED IMPACT TO ANOTHER EXAMPLE OF THE ELECTRIC BLUE AND ORANGE COMBINATION.

Vibrant schemes

While complementary schemes are based around the natural vibrancy of complementary pairs, they need not make your eyes water. Vibrant combinations, however, set out to be a shock to the system. These intense, full-on schemes are not for the faint-hearted but they do deliver an incredible sense of *joie de vivre* and an infectious delight in colour for its own sake.

Many vibrant schemes are based around colours that are said to clash: think bright red and pink with a touch of emerald green or cobalt blue in the detail, or intense turquoise paired with magenta. Most of us would find it tiring to live in surroundings where every surface was decorated in such an in-your-face way, but you can still enjoy the vitality of these combinations by restricting them to soft furnishings, for example, and keeping backgrounds neutral or more restrained.

Another way to achieve a certain edginess in a palette is to make use of tertiary colours, which are those that hover on the cusp of one colour and another. Many of these shades, which include turquoise blue, yellow-green, magenta and orange-red, look very different under changing light conditions, and this can give them a luminous quality that can be particularly evocative and atmospheric.

LEFT: SHOCKING PINK ADDS ZEST TO A WHITE KITCHEN. FLUORESCENT COLOURS ARE ESPECIALLY EYE-CATCHING.

FAR LEFT: FUCHSIA AND PURPLE SEATING DISPLAY A LOVE OF COLOUR FOR ITS OWN SAKE. THE WHITE BACKGROUND PREVENTS THE EFFECT FROM BECOMING TOO OVERWHELMING.

Graphic schemes

The quintessential graphic scheme is the refined, formal pairing of black and white, which occurs countless times in decoration, from the classic black and white chequered floor to the striking contemporary black and white furnishing fabrics produced by designers such as Timney Fowler of London. The combination, which displays maximum contrast, has undeniable power – think of chairs and sofas upholstered in black leather against an ivory white background, or black slate walls offset with white ceramic bathroom fixtures, or a collection of black and white prints or photographs displayed on a wall.

You can soften the severity of black and white, while still retaining its impact, by adding almost any other colour into the mix, either as an accent, focal point or background shade. Combining black and white with naturals and neutrals expresses sophisticated urban chic. Textural variety will also help to ring the changes, with contrasts of glass, steel and polished stone giving depth to the basic scheme.

Graphic schemes that rely heavily on primary colours also make bold statements. An obvious point of reference is the work of the Dutch artist Piet Mondrian, whose compositions of white squares and rectangles divided by strong black lines and interspersed with blocks of primary colour are instantly familiar. The modern decorative style hi-tech, which first saw commercial and industrial fittings and materials used in a domestic setting, was also typically expressed in primary colours, mediated by grey.

ABOVE: A BOLD RED AND WHITE STRIPED RUG LENDS A STRONG GRAPHIC ELEMENT TO A RETRO-STYLE KITCHEN.

RIGHT: BLACK AND WHITE IS THE CLASSIC GRAPHIC COMBINATION, HERE GIVEN EXTRA IMPACT BY THE LARGE SCALE OF THE PATTERN.

Living areas

We tend to put more thought and effort into the way living areas are decorated and furnished, simply because these are places where we are more likely to entertain friends and family. At the same time, pressure on space means that living areas often have to serve other functions as well. A colour scheme alone will not reconcile the challenges of spatial planning, but it can lend a sense of coherence to parts of a home where different activities take place.

■ Think about when you use the living room most and choose your colours accordingly. Certain shades look best in natural light; softer, moodier tones may be a better bet if you use the room more in the evening.

■ Much will depend on whether you prefer to keep books and CDs on open shelving or concealed from view. Open displays are visually busy and contribute both colour and pattern to an interior, which tends to mean that background colours should be more muted in comparison.

■ Sofas are large and dominant items of furniture. Upholstered in a strong solid colour, they can inject a note of vitality into an otherwise neutral scheme. Alternatively, if space is limited, you can diminish the impact of a large sofa by opting for white or neutral coloured upholstery material.

■ A wall picked out in a strong colour can signal a change of use within an open-plan space.

LEFT: WARM, NATURAL TONES DOMINATE IN THIS OPEN-PLAN LIVING AREA. THE SLATE COLOURED MEZZANINE LEVEL MINIMIZES ITS BULK AND APPEARS TO RECEDE.

ABOVE: AN OPEN-PLAN AREA COMPRISING KITCHEN, EATING AND LIVING SPACES SEES THE KITCHEN PICKED OUT IN A VIVID RED TO ANNOUNCE THE SHIFT OF ACTIVITY.

Kitchens

With its connotations of purity and hygiene, white has played a significant role in kitchen decoration over the years and plain white remains the first choice for many when choosing a kitchen. Pairing white with blue, though, creates a classic combination that manages to suggest both freshness and cosy domesticity. Equally popular is the wholesome country kitchen look, a style that relies heavily on the earthy and natural tones of cream, biscuit and terracotta, more often than not expressed in materials such as wood, tile and stone. Recently, contemporary kitchen décor has become a lot bolder, with backgrounds and even large-scale appliances displaying intense pure colours such as siren red, tangerine and midnight blue.

- The kitchen is a functional place first and foremost. Introduce colour sparingly to keep attention focused on the task at hand. One strong colour, or tones of the same colour, is generally enough. Allow plenty of breathing space between blocks of colour.
- Incidental kitchen displays, such as bowls of fresh fruit and vegetables, coloured crockery and enamelled kitchen equipment can contribute a great sense of vitality, even where backgrounds are subdued.
- It is easy to repaint walls if you are tired of the colour and relatively easy to refinish cupboard doors. A brightly coloured appliance or vivid flooring is a more permanent feature, however, and must be chosen carefully.

LEFT: VASES AND COLOURED GLASSWARE MAKE A VIBRANT KITCHEN DISPLAY THAT IS EASY TO CHANGE.

RIGHT: A RESTRAINED COLOUR SCHEME, FEATURING WHITE, CREAM AND TONES OF BROWN, MAKES THE MOST OF NATURAL LIGHT IN THIS KITCHEN.

Eating areas

Sitting down to eat a meal with family or friends should be an enjoyable social occasion. Choosing colours for eating areas means thinking about creating the right mood for the appreciation of both food and company. Here the focus is very much on the table, and backgrounds should not compete for attention. A comparison with restaurants, cafés and other food outlets can be instructive – fast-food chains, for example, often make use of bright primaries to keep people on the move, while more upmarket restaurants, where people expect to linger and savour the experience, will feature moodier, more sophisticated palettes to promote a sense of intimacy and hospitality.

- Where an eating area forms part of an open-plan space, you can pick out a wall in a plane of colour to signal the shift of activity.
- Colours from the warm end of the spectrum are enclosing and draw people together. A rich red is often featured as the background colour in the formal dining rooms of the past.
- An earthy palette based around grey-browns, ochres and pale cream can be very effective in a country setting.
- Where backgrounds are neutral, think about introducing colour in table settings by using coloured crockery and glassware, as well as napkins and tablecloths.

ABOVE: TABLE LINEN AND COLOURFUL CROCKERY AND GLASSWARE MAKE CHEERFUL DISPLAYS IN EATING AREAS WHERE BACKGROUNDS ARE MORE RESTRAINED.

LEFT: A PREDOMINANTLY RED PAINTING SERVES TO ANCHOR AN EATING AREA WITHIN AN OPEN-PLAN SPACE. COLOURED EAMES CHAIRS AND PANTONE MUGS ADD VITALITY.

Bedrooms

As the place where we begin each day, the bedroom is one area of the home where it is particularly important to choose colours according to the quality of natural light. This is all the more true where the bedroom has a single aspect. In north- or east-facing rooms (the opposite in the Southern Hemisphere) light will be inherently chilly, which means that you will need a colour scheme in which warm colours predominate. South- or west-facing rooms are much warmer and sunnier and can take cooler palettes as a consequence. Even where you are opting for a neutral scheme you need to take orientation into account. There is a significant difference, for example, between a creamy white and an icy white.

■ Tertiary colours are a good way of introducing colour interest into a bedroom without undermining any sense of relaxation.

■ The bed is a large and dominant piece of furniture, which means that the colour of bed linen or of an upholstered bedhead, for example, will contribute significantly to a decorative scheme. Where backgrounds are neutral, a brightly coloured blanket or throw can inject a little vitality.

■ If you opt for a natural or neutral palette, textural variety will help to prevent the overall look from being too bland. Soft furnishings are the easiest way to add texture: embroidered bedlinen, cushions and throws, or woven or deep-pile rugs are all effective.

ABOVE: TEXTURAL VARIETY FROM THE USE OF DIFFERENT MATERIALS GIVES DEPTH TO A NEUTRAL SCHEME.

RIGHT: COOL COLOURS, SUCH AS BLUES AND GREYS, ARE IDEAL FOR BEDROOMS THAT ARE SOUTH- OR WEST-FACING.

Bathrooms

Not so long ago bathrooms used to be seen as fairly clinical places and decorated in a relatively subdued and no-nonsense fashion. Today, as bathrooms increasingly serve as havens of well-being, colour, along with its power to evoke moods – whether of revitalisation or relaxation – has come to the forefront.

- Bathrooms are essentially fitted spaces in which the layout is determined by the position of the necessary fixtures and fittings. Unless your bathroom is very large, it is best to opt for a colour scheme where a single colour predominates in order to provide unity.
- White remains the norm for sanitary ware for a good reason. Colours go in and out of fashion – think of avocado bathroom suites – and it is much easier, cheaper and less disruptive to update a background than to change fittings and fixtures.
- Various shades of blue, blue-green and blue-grey are popular for bathroom décor, which is not surprising given their association with watery environments. Blue is also naturally space-enhancing, which helps if your bathroom is on the small side.
- Small bathrooms and cloakrooms can be decorated in strong shades that you might find too tiring to live with in larger doses.
- Try to avoid over-coordinating bathroom accessories and linen. It can look twee.

ABOVE: A PANEL OF RICH, DEEP RED DEFINES A SHOWERING AREA WITHIN A WET ROOM. SLATTED HARDWOOD PROVIDES WARMTH UNDERFOOT.

LEFT: RANDOMLY PATTERNED BLUE MOSAIC HAS A UNIFYING EFFECT CLADDING BATHROOM WALLS.

Children's rooms

Children's rooms are naturally busy, with plenty of brightly coloured toys on display, which is a strong argument in favour of keeping walls relatively plain and neutral. You can introduce stronger colour in the choice of flooring without the effect becoming too overwhelming.

Neutral backgrounds can also help you keep pace with each successive stage in your child's development. Using colour for accents and focal points will help you ring the changes more easily and economically.

- As with adult bedrooms, pay attention to the quality of light and choose colours accordingly. This is particularly important since children tend to spend more time in their rooms during the day than adults do.
- Graphic schemes, featuring strong combinations of primary colours, or red, white and blue, often work well in children's rooms.
- Even small children are naturally stimulated by colour and soon come to have their own likes and dislikes. Within reason, allow children some say in the way that their room is decorated. Colourful soft furnishings, such as duvet covers and curtains, are cheap and easy to change.
- Teenagers will almost certainly want to put their own stamp on their surroundings, and even if this takes the form of lurid or Gothic colour schemes, it all about expressing their sense of identity.

ABOVE: A STRIPED RUG DISPLAYS BRIGHT, GRAPHIC COLOUR IN A CHILD'S ROOM. YELLOW HAS BEEN PICKED OUT AS A BACKGROUND SHADE.

RIGHT: LIME GREEN MAKES A VIVID BACKDROP TO COLOURFUL DISPLAYS OF TOYS, GAMES AND BOOKS.

Halls, entrances & stairs

Areas of transition such as halls, entrances and stairs are typically experienced only fleetingly as we move about the home. As linking spaces, they are also about views, since we may catch glimpses of them from other rooms.

The temptation is often to treat these transitional spaces in a neutral fashion, which can be a sensible strategy when the areas they connect make strong decorative statements of their own. The opposite approach, though, can be surprisingly effective. Strong colour in hallways – on the walls or in the form of a stair carpet, runner or painted treads — can serve as a vivid, optimistic thread running through your home and tying all its different spaces together. Colour also makes a positive first impression at the entrance.

It is often best, however, to keep things relatively simple. One positive colour, offset with black and white or natural shades, has graphic strength and punchiness. A palette of three or four colours and tones, such as you might use in a living area, is a little too subtle for areas where you are not going to linger long. As with any other area, pay attention to natural light. In older properties, hallways may be relatively dark in comparison to living areas and might benefit from warmer colours.

LEFT: A WALL-MOUNTED RETRO-STYLE COAT RACK PROVIDES THE EXCUSE FOR THE DISPLAY OF BRIGHT COLOUR IN A NEUTRAL HALLWAY.

RIGHT: SINCE HALLWAYS ARE AREAS OF TRANSITION, THEY CAN BE GOOD PLACES TO APPLY STRONG DECORATIVE STATEMENTS.

INTRODUCTION
UNDERSTANDING COLOUR
COLOUR SCHEMES
PRACTICAL COLOUR

Basic considerations

Once you have come up with a colour scheme for your home or for a particular area within it, the next stage is to turn your colour ideas into reality. These days, bright colour is not limited to paint, fabric and other forms of applied decoration, as it chiefly was in the recent past. Almost any material, fixture or fitting is available in a range of shades, widening the scope considerably. Practical colour is essentially about choosing materials and finishes.

- If you are hesitant about introducing colour in large doses, either stick to small-scale applications, such as accents, accessories and displays until your confidence grows, or choose finishes such as paint that are relatively quick and economical to change.
- If you are unsure about painting a wall or room in a particular colour, try painting a large panel of card in your chosen colour, pin it to your wall and live with it for a few days or until you are convinced it is the right one.
- It is important to bear in mind that colour is no substitute for performance. If turning colour ideas into reality means choosing materials for surfaces and finishes, bear in mind that these elements have practical as well as decorative roles to play. You may have your heart set on a beautiful blue fabric to upholster your sofa, but unless the weave is robust enough, it will not be able to stand up to the job it has to do.

ABOVE: WITH MANY MATERIALS AND FINISHES, COLOUR VARIES SLIGHTLY FROM BATCH TO BATCH. ALWAYS ENSURE YOU HAVE ENOUGH TO COMPLETE THE JOB.

RIGHT: DARK WOODEN FLOOR BOARDS AND BLUE-GREY WALLS ARE OFFSET BY THE WHITE CEILING AND LIGHTER DADO PANELLING.

Material character

Colour is just one element of the decorative palette. In practice, colour, pattern and texture work together in a way that engages all our senses, not merely sight. A wooden floor, for example, contributes not only a rich natural shade, but also patterning in the grain and the lines of the boards, as well as its sound and feel when you walk across it.

When colour schemes are based around tones of one shade, or on simple pairings, textural variety can inject the necessary degree of character and vitality to prevent the effect from being bland. This is particularly valuable in the case of neutral schemes, which are naturally quieter and less likely to turn up the emotional temperature. While smooth plastered walls painted cream and an expanse of beige carpet might send you nodding off to sleep, for example, cream painted brickwork and natural fibre flooring starts to become more interesting because textural contrast is playing a greater role in the décor.

You also need to bear in mind that colour is significantly affected by finish, because light will be reflected in a different manner according to whether the surface is matt, smooth or shiny. This is also something to consider if the material you have chosen for a particular application needs to be sealed, varnished or otherwise treated to enhance wear-resistance.

LEFT: THE CONTRAST IN MATERIAL CHARACTER BETWEEN SMOOTH PLASTER, EXPOSED BRICKWORK AND THE OPEN HARDWOOD STAIRCASE IS THE HEART OF THIS SCHEME.

ABOVE: NATURAL STONE AND WOOD DISPLAY PATTERNING AND GRAINING IN THEIR SURFACES THAT ADDS DEPTH OF CHARACTER TO RESTRAINED COLOUR SCHEMES.

Paint

Paint is a simple, direct and affordable means of enjoying colour, with the added bonus that it is easy to change if you find that you are unhappy with a particular shade, or grow tired of it more quickly than you had imagined. Yet while paint is a cheaper decorating choice, it is important to opt for quality and pay a little more if necessary. Good quality paint has better coverage, is easier to apply and often contains more pigment, so that colours are truer and richer.

Types of paint

- Water-based paint, or emulsion, is the standard finish for plastered walls.
- Vinyl emulsions, which have increased water-resistance, are produced for areas such as kitchens and bathrooms where humidity can be a problem.
- Oil-based paints include gloss and eggshell (also known as silk, satin or semi-gloss). Because they wear better and last longer than emulsion, such finishes are recommended for woodwork, cabinetry and doors.
- Specialist paints are available for painting metalwork, floorboards and tiles.
- Traditional paints such as limewash and distemper can be used for an authentic finish in period buildings.
- Eco paints, composed of organic pigments, binders and solvents, have improved dramatically in recent years, both in terms of colour range and ease of application. They do not contain plastics and permit walls to breathe, and they are also hypoallergenic.

ABOVE: PAINT IS ONE OF THE CHEAPEST AND MOST IMMEDIATE WAYS OF ADDING THE LIFT OF COLOUR TO YOUR SURROUNDINGS. ROYAL BLUE WALLS HERE MAKE A STRONG STATEMENT.

RIGHT: THINK ABOUT CONTRASTING FINISHES. THESE BANDS OF MOODY COLOUR HAVE BEEN ACHIEVED IN BOTH MATT AND SHEEN PAINT.

Continued

Paint

Points to consider

- Always take the time to prepare surfaces properly before starting to paint. Wash, brush or vacuum to get rid of dirt and loose debris. Fill cracks and holes with proprietary filler, allow to dry and sand down, repeating if necessary. If your walls are really battered and you cannot afford to replaster, think about lining or cross-lining to give a smooth, even surface for decoration. If woodwork is clogged with layers of old paint, use a blowtorch or chemical stripper to restore the crispness of the mouldings.

- A single coat of paint gives a wall an instant face-lift, but a much better result will be achieved if you apply two or more layers. Ideally you should use a primer, followed by an undercoat, followed by a topcoat of your chosen colour.

- Oil and water do not mix. Never mix oil-based and water-based paint on the same surface.

- A good space-enhancing strategy is to paint mouldings, trims and features such as radiators the same colour as the walls.

- To paint a room, start with the ceiling and work away from the main source of natural light. Then paint the walls in vertical sections, again working away from the main source of natural light. Finally paint doors, window frames and skirting boards.

ABOVE: IT IS USUAL TO CHOOSE VINYL EMULSION PAINT, WHICH HAS INCREASED WATER-RESISTANCE, FOR KITCHENS AND BATHROOMS.

LEFT: COLOUR CHANGES IN DIFFERENT LIGHT CONDITIONS SO IT IS ADVISABLE TO BUY SAMPLE POTS IN A RANGE OF LIGHTER AND DARKER TONES AND PAINT TEST PATCHES ON A WALL TO ASSESS HOW A COLOUR LOOKS.

Paper

Wallpaper is synonymous with pattern, which in turn is rooted in colour combination. While you may have chosen a décor where a single colour or graphic contrast predominates, your choice of wallpaper will effectively provide you with a ready-made colour scheme for the rest of the room. The exception are textural papers made of woven fibres such as grass, sisal, jute and rattan, which are much more subtle and self-effacing.

In recent years, wallpaper has shed its conventional image to become the height of interior fashion, with many leading designers producing exciting contemporary designs in bold colours and large-scale motifs. At the same time, traditional, floral and geometric designs remain popular in the mass market, many with matching borders and friezes, and in robust vinyl-coated versions specially produced for use in kitchens and bathrooms.

Wallpaper does not need to be restricted for use on walls. You could use wallpaper inside cupboards or a wardrobe to give an element of surprise. If you are feeling creative, almost anything that can be stuck to the wall – such as posters and maps – can be collaged to make an original backdrop.

Paper tends to be more expensive than paint – much more expensive in the case of high-quality or hand-blocked varieties – and paper-hanging requires more skill to achieve a successful result. If you are unsure about your DIY abilities, it is best to hire a decorator to do the job for you.

ABOVE: BEFORE YOU COMMIT YOURSELF TO A FINAL CHOICE, PIN UP A DROP OF WALLPAPER AND LIVE WITH IT FOR A WHILE TO ASSESS ITS IMPACT.

RIGHT: THE COLOURS OF THIS BAMBOO-PATTERNED DESIGN ARE ECHOED IN THE UPHOLSTERY AND FLOORING.

Continued

Paper

Points to consider

- Prepare the surface properly for optimum results. Wallpaper is best pasted over lining paper and walls should be cross-lined (papered vertically and horizontally) if they are in really poor condition.
- Always buy enough paper for the job, allowing extra for wastage.
- Follow the manufacturer's instructions and use the recommended paste.
- The standard procedure is to paste the back of a drop of paper, allow a few minutes for the paper to expand and then apply it to the wall, smoothing out any wrinkles. Some decorators also apply a thin coat of paste to the wall. With some modern wallpapers, the paste is applied directly to the wall instead, which means that all you have to do is position the drops of paper correctly.
- The first drop of paper should be hung in the corner of the room nearest the main window, so that you work away from the direction of natural light. If the paper features a large-scale pattern, however, you should centre the first sheet in the middle of the wall or above a focal point, such as a fireplace, and work towards the corners of the room to avoid drawing attention to interruptions in the pattern's repeat.

LEFT: LIKE PAINT, WALLPAPER CAN BE USED TO CREATE A FEATURE WALL - ONE OF THE BEST WAYS OF LIVING WITH A BUSY DESIGN.

ABOVE: WALLPAPER-HANGING IS LARGELY A PROFESSIONAL JOB - THIS DESIGN, WITH ITS BOLD STRIPES, REQUIRES PERFECT POSITIONING SO THAT THE LINES ARE STRAIGHT.

Fabric

Generally cheaper and less permanent than many other materials used in decoration, fabric is an accessible way of introducing colour to the home. Most types of soft furnishings – such as rugs, upholstery, cushion covers, curtains, and bed and bath linen – are easy to change if you want to put a fresh face on things or respond to the seasons. Swapping dark loose covers for white or light-toned ones will instantly give a room more of a summery look.

Fabric brings depth to colour schemes because of its inherent texture, which may be expressed in an overt weave or nap, or in the way that light filters through it. Glazed cotton chintz, for example, makes colours appear sharp and crisp, while sheer or translucent fabrics hanging at the window can tint the light to create a soft, evocative ambience.

Choosing fabrics with a motif is an effective way of incorporating pattern in a décor. You may wish to source a pattern that brings together the main colours of your decorative scheme, or that serves as a focal point or accent in a neutral setting. An alternative approach is to choose a patterned fabric first and base a decorative scheme around the colours it displays.

ABOVE: A STRIPED FLATWEAVE RUG AND SPOTTED CUSHION COVERS PROVIDE TOUCHES OF ACCENT COLOURS IN AN OTHERWISE NEUTRAL SCHEME.

RIGHT: A SUBTLE AND SOPHISTICATED COMBINATION OF MOODY BLUES, PURPLES AND BROWNS IS DISPLAYED BY THE SOFA UPHOLSTERY AND CUSHION COVERS.

PANTONE®
286 C

Continued

Fabric

Points to consider

- Bear in mind how you are going to use a fabric. Upholstery materials, particularly if the upholstery is fitted, need to be heavy and robust to stand up to wear and tear. If the fabric crumples when you gather it or if the cut edges unravel easily, it is probably too light to be used for upholstery.

- Cushion covers and filmy window drapery do not take the same kind of punishment as upholstery, which means that you can use materials that are lighter in weight.

- Think about maintenance. Upholstery can be treated to make it more resistant to stains.

- You do not need much in the way of sewing skills to make cushion covers, or simple tie-headed or gathered curtains. Lined curtains, as well as those with pleated or tailored headings, require more expertise.

- Many furnishing fabrics include a percentage of synthetic fibres to add strength and promote fire-retardance. When you are choosing bed or bath linen, however, natural materials always feel better next to the skin because they are absorbent.

- Think laterally and investigate the possibilities of using fabrics from sources other than the soft furnishing department. Saris, suit fabrics, ethnic textiles, or remnants that you might have picked up in a market or second-hand shop, often display vivid colour combinations and interesting patterns.

ABOVE: CHOOSE THE RIGHT FABRIC FOR THE JOB IT HAS TO DO. UPHOLSTERY MATERIALS MUST BE ROBUST AND HARD-WEARING.

LEFT: SOFT FURNISHINGS, FROM BED LINEN TO CUSHION COVERS, ARE AN EASY WAY TO INTRODUCE COLOUR INTO YOUR SURROUNDINGS.

Flooring

Coloured flooring is a great way of giving different spaces a sense of uplift and identity, particularly in contemporary open-plan layouts where the rest of the décor is relatively restrained. Although the floor represents a substantial amount of surface area, even a strong colour is less likely to dominate, simply because it is underfoot.

As with other surfaces and finishes, you cannot base your choice of flooring on looks alone. Practical issues, such as wear and tear, ease of maintenance, resilience, comfort and installation will also come into play.

- If your home is on the small side, extending the same flooring throughout is space-enhancing and unifying. Different flooring materials that are similar in tone will have the same effect. In an open-plan kitchen-diner, for example, you could combine pale wooden flooring for the eating area with light coloured tiles for the kitchen.

- Colour is great for floors in hallways and stairs, and will serve as a vivid ribbon linking areas together and leading the eye onwards. On the stairs, for example, a red carpet, treads and risers painted in a bright colour, or a long striped runner can be very striking.

- If you do not want to commit to coloured flooring on a permanent basis, carpet runners, or area and scatter rugs of all descriptions, are easy ways to deliver colour.

LEFT: WOODEN FLOORING COMES IN A RANGE OF NATURAL TONES THAT CAN BE FURTHER ENHANCED OR EXTENDED BY STAINING, VARNISHING OR PAINTING.

RIGHT: BOTH RUBBER AND POURED RESIN FLOORING COMES IN AN INCREDIBLY WIDE RANGE OF COLOURS.

Continued

Flooring

Materials

- **Rubber** For bright, saturated colour, rubber is hard to beat. One manufacturer of rubber tile and sheet guarantees to match any Pantone colour swatch; off the peg, the breadth of colour choice is vast. Warm, resilient and very long-lasting, rubber is a highly practical floor. Textured finishes are less slippery.

- **Linoleum** Although its colours tend to be softer and slightly mottled, linoleum also comes in a good range of colours and in tile or sheet form. It is a high-quality, wholly natural product that is warm, hygienic, durable, resistant to stains, and hypoallergenic, which makes it a good choice for allergy sufferers.

- **Ceramic tile** Available in a huge range of colours, patterns, sizes and shapes, ceramic tile is a practical flooring for hard-working areas such as halls, bathrooms and kitchens, where water-resistance is important.

- **Vinyl** Coloured, patterned or designed to simulate a natural material, vinyl comes in both sheet and tile formats. The better grades are longer-lasting and more expensive.

- **Paint** Wooden floors can be stripped and sanded, then painted or stained. Stain soaks into the grain and gives a softer effect than paint. For areas of light traffic, oil-based gloss paint or eggshell will do; otherwise choose hard-wearing floor or yacht paint.

LEFT: RUGS ARE A GREAT WAY OF BRINGING A DASH OF COLOUR AND PATTERN TO AN INTERIOR AND ARE EASY TO CHANGE IF YOU FANCY A DIFFERENT MOOD.

ABOVE: EXTENDING THE SAME FLOORING THROUGH DIFFERENT AREAS OF THE HOME, PARTICULARLY IN OPEN PLAN LAYOUTS, IS A WAY OF ACHIEVING VISUAL UNITY.

Lighting

Both natural and artificial lighting have a great impact on the way we perceive colours. How colours appear under conditions of bright natural light is generally taken to be the benchmark, but even natural light can alter the way the same colour appears, depending on orientation and light levels. In the case of artificial light, the difference is even more marked.

Types of light source

- The most familiar artificial light source in the home is the tungsten bulb, which is soon to be discontinued in many parts of the world due to its extreme lack of energy efficiency. That aside, what most people value about this light source is its visual warmth. The light produced by tungsten has a yellowish cast, which is both flattering for the complexion and innately hospitable.
- Halogen, another relatively common light source, produces a much whiter light than tungsten, which is better at colour rendering. This means that colours viewed under halogen will appear closer to the way they do under natural light. For this reason, halogen is useful where you need to make colour judgements – in working areas, for example, or in kitchens.
- From the point of view of colour rendering, fluorescent light is more problematic. Although improvements have been made in recent years, fluorescent light tends to have a greenish cast, which can have a very deadening effect on colour schemes.

ABOVE: LIGHT SHINING THROUGH PANES OF STAINED GLASS GIVES COLOURS A JEWEL-LIKE INTENSITY.

RIGHT: ALL-WHITE DÉCOR IS FRESH AND UPLIFTING WHERE THE QUALITY OF NATURAL LIGHT IS GOOD.

Continued

Lighting

Coloured light

Combining light with colour can be quite magical and evocative in its effect, particularly as an accent or decorative focal point. At the very simplest, you can 'colour' light by shading a bulb with a coloured transparent or translucent material, in the same way that natural light can be tinted by stained glass in windows, transoms or door panels. The stained leaded glass Tiffany lamp is a classic example, but there are many contemporary versions.

Extending the same idea further, panels of coloured translucent Perspex or glass can be fitted to units or the sides of a bathtub with backlighting behind them. In such cases, the light source needs to be fluorescent, which emits very little heat and so is safe to be used in close proximity to other materials.

Energy efficient LEDs (light-emitting diodes), widely believed to be the light source of the future, are increasingly making an appearance in the home. Coloured LEDs can be inset into wall panels, flooring, the base of stairs or even in bathtubs to provide eye-catching colour effects. They are incredibly long-lasting, with lifespans of thousands of hours, which means that they can be used in such installations without you having to worry about changing them.

ABOVE: DIFFERENT LIGHT SOURCES HAVE DIFFERENT COLOUR CASTS. HALOGEN IS CLOSEST TO DAYLIGHT; TUNGSTEN HAS A YELLOWISH GLOW.

LEFT: BACKLIGHTING A PERSPEX OR GLASS PANEL ENCLOSING A BATH CREATES AN EVOCATIVE MOOD OF RELAXATION.

Fittings & fixtures

The contemporary home, where there is often a great deal of pressure on space and a need to maximize floor area, tends to include many fitted elements and fixtures, from built-in wardrobes to walls of shelving and other storage features. In many cases, you do not want to draw particular attention to such elements – especially if your home is on the small side – and the best strategy is often to paint them white or some other neutral shade to make them more self-effacing; if the walls are coloured, paint them to match the background so that they blend in.

Kitchen and bathroom cabinetry, however, offers much more scope for colour expression. Fitted units come in a wide range of colours and finishes these days, from strong primaries to more subtle shades. As with coloured appliances, you need to be sure that you are prepared to live with the colour for a decent length of time. This is particularly true if the units are made of a veneered or laminate material that cannot subsequently be refinished. Otherwise you can fit wood or MDF doors to a basic carcase and decorate them yourself. When you tire of the colour or want to redecorate the room, you can then paint them a different shade.

ABOVE: WHITE IS NO LONGER THE STANDARD OPTION FOR KITCHEN APPLIANCES AND CABINETRY.

RIGHT: DEEP BLUE KITCHEN UNITS MAKE A GOOD COMBINATION WITH THE STAINLESS STEEL RANGE.

Display

If you are unsure how to make an impact with colour, putting together displays will help you to practice with different combinations and the results can be delightfully impromptu.

When you create a display, you are inviting the eye to linger, so choose a location that is relatively prominent, such as a mantelpiece, the centre of a table, or shelving that is at eye level. The same is true of displays that consist of framed pictures, photographs or posters. Grouping objects together always has more impact than dotting them about the place.

Displays are more effective if there is a theme of some kind to draw everything together. It may be a specific period of vintage ceramics or it may be a type of object; equally it may be colour. While coordination can be too bland a strategy for a decorative scheme as a whole, it is highly effective for displays and collections. Items can be quite disparate in type and origin, but provided they are all the same colour, the overall effect will be very arresting.

LEFT: BLUE AND GREEN GLASSWARE MAKES AN EVOCATIVE DISPLAY LINED UP ON A WINDOWSILL.

ABOVE: BOOKSHELVES CONTRIBUTE INCIDENTAL PATTERN AND COLOUR, WHILE MANTELPIECES ARE NATURAL PLACES FOR THE DISPLAY OF DECORATIVE OBJECTS AND FAVOURITE THINGS.

Continued

Display

Points to consider

- Where the basic decorative scheme is neutral or natural, colourful displays are essential. You do not have to amass objects that show every colour in the rainbow, but one or two largish items in one or two strong colours will inject a sense of personality and character.
- By contrast, if there is already a lot of colour in the room, exercise an element of restraint with displays, and restrict yourself to objects that match in tone with the overall scheme or make a simple contrast to it.
- Enhance the appeal of coloured glassware by backlighting it or arranging it on a window ledge where light can shine through.

- Broaden your definition of display to include everyday items such as fresh fruit and vegetables, packaging, pots and pans, and utensils, all of which can contribute colour accents to kitchens when left out on view. The spines of books or CDs on shelves make a similar contribution to living areas.
- Changing displays from time to time is a good way of injecting vitality into your surroundings and putting a fresh face on things.
- Hallways and stairs also make good places for display. A collection of pictures on a wall flanking a stair, or a group of ceramics on a window ledge, will retain their charm for longer because you see them only in passing.

ABOVE: A PAIR OF WHITE SHELVES CANTILEVERED FROM THE WALL PROVIDES A PLACE TO SHOWCASE CERAMICS AND OTHER DECORATIVE OBJECTS.

RIGHT: EVEN FUNCTIONAL DISPLAYS, SUCH AS BATH LINEN STACKED ON SHELVES LINING A RECESS, CONTRIBUTE PERSONALITY AND CHARACTER.

Index